Fun Things To Do

Maureen Maddren

Illustrated by Joyce Tuhill

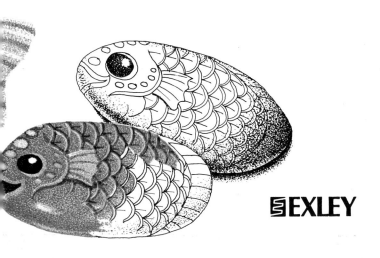

EXLEY

Also from Exley by Maureen Maddren:
Free Stuff For Kids
Play As We Go
Rainy Day Fun and Games

Published in Great Britain in 1990 by
Exley Publications Ltd
16 Chalk Hill, Watford, Herts WD1 4BN, United Kingdom.

Copyright © Exley Publications Ltd, 1990

British Library Cataloguing in Publication Data
Maddren, Maureen.
 Fun things to do.
 1. Amusements – Juvenile literature.
 I. Title.
 790.1'922   GV1203

ISBN 1-85015-081-8

Designed by Nick Maddren.
Illustrations by Joyce Tuhill.
Typeset by Brush Off Studios, St Albans, Herts AL3 4PH.
Printed and bound in Hungary.

CONTENTS

INTRODUCTION

FUN THINGS TO DO will show you how to make lots of exciting, creative things out of inexpensive materials, most of which can be found around the house.

There are outdoor things to build like bird tables, nesting boxes and ponds; you can make and fly kites, study the wildlife that lives around your home or plant a tree.

Why not take up a new hobby: collect stamps, coins, shells or cheese labels; delve into your past and discover what your ancestors did, then draw up a family tree; make sculptures using wire and papier mâché or press flowers to use in a variety of ways. Give new life to your clothes by learning new dyeing techniques, appliqué fun shapes onto well-worn denims or make some new accessories to brighten up your wardrobe.

Learn to make fun things from paper; giant hang-ups, decorative mobiles to catch the light in a bedroom or hallway or large paper flowers to fill a dark corner.

Now if you feel like some refreshment, go into the kitchen and rustle up a quick snack, a delicious pancake or speedy spaghetti bolognese, then wash it down with a smooth choc-mint sizzle.

All the instructions and recipes are easy to follow; just collect all the materials and ingredients together and make making things FUN!

Kites

Kites are still very much a feature of life in the Far East, where on certain festival days, whole families will turn out with their own individual models. The designs are usually very elaborate and are made to look like butterflies, birds and fish. They may take a little longer to make than the traditional geometric-shaped kites that we know best, but the finished product is well worth the effort.

Cutter or traditional kite

For this you need two sticks; one must be half as long again as the other, so that if the shorter one is 16in (40cm), the longer one will be 24in (60cm). Lay the sticks at right angles to each other so that the shorter one lies a third of the way down across the longer one. Glue them together then bind the join with sticky tape. Tie a length of string 1¼in (6cm) in from the end of one stick and then run it round the ends of the other sticks in turn to make your diamond shape. Choose some paper with a fairly distinctive design – it could be wallpaper, wrapping paper or even a poster – or paint on a motif of your own. With the right side of the paper facing down, lay the kite frame on top and trim the paper out to the same shape, allowing a 1in (2.5cm) overlapping edge. Turn this edge in and glue it down over the string. Make a tail by twisting some small pieces of paper (tissues are ideal), into bow shapes and tying them onto a piece of string 72in (180cm) long. This is then attached to the base of the kite. The flying line will also be tied on at this point. You can wind the line itself round a stiff cardboard tube, making sure the end is tightly secured to the tube or you may lose the kite!

The carp

This is a very popular design in Japan and is easy to construct as it is the only one that does not need a frame. Simply cut a carp shape out through two thicknesses of tissue or other light-weight paper leaving a wide opening for the mouth. Glue all the sides together except the mouth and tail so that

you get a windsock effect when it is flying. Attach a circle of wire to the mouth to keep it open and tie your flying line to this. The carp is quite a difficult kite to fly and needs a good blast of air to get it going.

The butterfly

The diagram right shows two different frame arrangements for butterfly kites. Model (A) requires short lengths of split bamboo (or stiff cardboard) to form the skeleton. Fold your paper in half – use a plain paper then you can paint a really dazzling design on it – and

These diagrams, a, b and c, show how the dowel or bamboo rods should be tied together to achieve the shapes illustrated above.

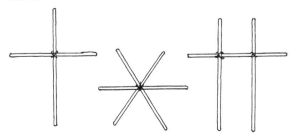

The dragonfly

Make a frame for the wings, as shown below (C), and cover it with tissue paper or something similar. The tail is made in sections so that it moves jerkily in the wind. Stick some pieces of paper to small strips of cardboard or bamboo and tie these loosely to each other with thread. Attach your flying line to the frame of the dragonfly.

cut out a half butterfly shape so that the fold forms the "spine" of the butterfly. Use sticky tape to secure the skeleton shape to the paper. Attach a piece of thread to the top and bottom of the central support and tie your flying line to the middle of it. Model (B) has two longer supports, curved to make the wing.

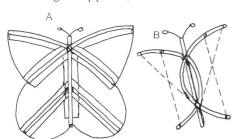

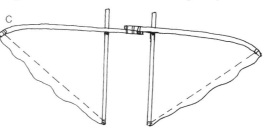

Fun Cards

Greetings cards are fun to make and they'll save you a fortune. You can make them for all sorts of occasions and they'll be appreciated far more than any you buy. We've illustrated ideas for four slightly unusual cards, but you can also make attractive cards using pressed flowers, potato prints and stencils.

Choirgirl card

This card could also be a robot (R2D2-type), angel, clown, a tree or Santa Claus going down a chimney pot.

Just fold the paper, draw the outline of the shape on one side of the card, then cut round the pencil line with the card still folded. Fill in the details and you have a card made in about five mintues.

Spaceman card

Try to think of something puzzling and enigmatic to write on the front of these cards so that the person receiving it will wonder what's inside. For instance, on this card you might say: "Hope your birthday reaches new heights" or "Best wishes for a brilliant lift-off to your birthday".

A Fold a rectangular piece of paper in half lengthways and cut off a section as shown.

B Fold down corner so that tip faces bottom right corner of card.

C Refold card so that this flap is now inside and will stand up as you open the card.

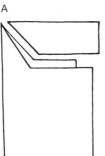

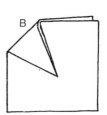

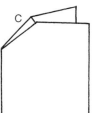

Frog card

Write your greeting inside the frog's mouth – something like "Hoppy Birthday" or "Hopping you'll get well soon". You can probably think of other ways of using this idea – the mouth could be a robin's beak for Christmas or a very toothy grin for a "Congratulations" card.

A Fold a rectangular piece of paper in half lengthways.

B Make a cut about a quarter of the way down the fold.

C Fold the paper in half widthways so that the cut is on the inside of the card. Gently ease the cut edges back so that the slit opens as the card closes.

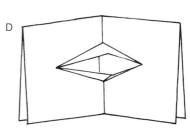

D Draw your design and write a message in the open "mouth".

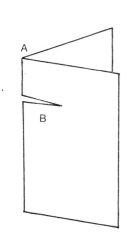

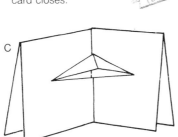

Cow card

There are lots of variations on this cow card: different animal faces, clown faces, two one-eyed monsters and so on.

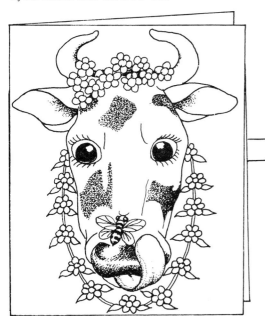

A Fold an A4 piece of paper in half and then half again to make the basic card shape.

B Cut two eyeholes in the front of the card.

C Cut two slots about ½in. (1.3cm) in from the two outer edges of the inside of the card. If you make two dots through the eyes you will find the correct position.

D Cut out a strip of paper and push it through the slots with the two ends on the inside of the card. Draw the eyes in and you can pull the strip from side to side to make the cow's eyes move.

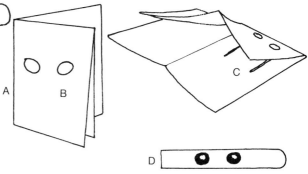

Bird-tables and nesting-boxes

The best way to encourage birds into your garden is by providing them with food, drink and shelter. Nesting-boxes and feeding-tables can be made from off-cuts of wood lying around in the garage. As long as their home is dry and cat-proof the birds will not mind if it doesn't win a design award.

The hanging bird table *(below)* could fix onto a bracket on the side or back wall of a house where the birds would not be disturbed

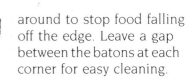

POSITIONING

There are some elementary rules on siting both nesting-boxes and feeding-tables and they are really quite obvious. Make sure that the local cat population does not have easy access to either. Bird-tables must be sited well away from fences and trees so that cats can't jump onto them. The pole that the bird-table is fixed to should be as smooth as possible; a rough surface would make climbing the pole an easy task for a cat. A metal pole would be ideal.

A roof on a bird-table is not absolutely essential but it will make life even more difficult for a determined and single-minded cat. Its major function, though, is to keep the rain out and prevent the food from becoming soggy or the table waterlogged. Birds may well use a roofed table as a shelter from a downpour of rain.

The tray should be at least 18x12in (45x30cm) with an inch-wide (2.5cm) baton all around to stop food falling off the edge. Leave a gap between the batons at each corner for easy cleaning.

POINTS TO NOTE

With nesting-boxes the main points to remember are: 1) It should be waterproof. 2) The entrance hole should be just big enough for the bird you want to attract – small birds will need a hole approximately 2.8cm/1⅛in in diameter (nestbox A). Use screws rather than nails for attaching the front of the box then you can easily remove it for cleaning purposes during the winter months. Some birds prefer a more open box, so you could cut the front panel of the box in half so that the bird has a veranda-type entry (nestbox B). 3) It should be in a sheltered position and should not face the wind. 4) Position the box not less than 1.5-2m/5-6ft off the ground.

WHAT FOOD?

To attract as wide a variety of birds as possible you will need to provide a varied menu. Some birds like insects, caterpillars and grubs, others enjoy fruit and berries, while a third group prefers nuts and seeds. You will find, though, that most birds will readily accept kitchen scraps and nearly all like peanuts. A good mixed menu for your bird-table would be bacon trimmings, cheese, suet, left-over scraps of cooked meat, cooked eggs, fruit, berries, nuts (but not salted ones), any seeds, boiled potato, stale cake crumbs, breadcrumbs and any grubs and maggots you can find. Don't put out any dehydrated food as it will swell up inside the birds and, if enough is eaten, will kill them.

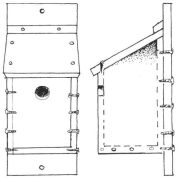

Above Cross-section of nesting box.

Right A: Bird box for small birds. B: For larger birds, cut off top half of front completely, still leaving it roofed, of course.

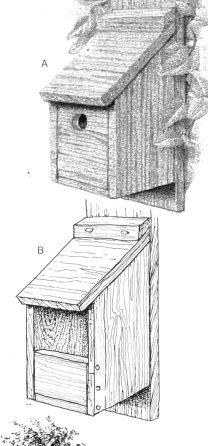

Peanuts in a purpose-built feeder or plastic mesh bag will provide welcome food for the birds.

You need feed only in the winter months as the birds will find their natural food once the weather is warmer.

Below An upturned bin lid makes an adequate bird bath. It also provides drinking water for the birds and a damp patch for other garden creatures beneath.

Appliqué

Give your denims a really individual look by sewing fabric shapes onto them. This is known as appliqué and is a craft that goes back many hundreds of years. Different shapes sewn on at random seem to be popular but we also like the idea of footprints walking down the back of a jacket (see opposite page). These are made in just a few easy stages as shown in the step-by-step diagrams below. If you use a bonded material, that is one which doesn't fray when it is cut, then it is not absolutely necessary to turn the edge under although it does give a neater finish. Felt is better left unhemmed as turning it under makes the edge too bulky. Don't restrict yourself to plain materials, buy up old dresses at rummage sales and go for a multi-patterned look.

When you have cut out and hemmed the foot shape, pin it in place on the jacket and then sew around the edge using a simple running stitch, or oversew the edge using either a contrasting or matching thread.

If you prefer, you can use a sewing machine to secure your motif to whatever article of clothing you choose, but it is often easier to do it by hand, particularly if you are appliquéing a design onto your jeans.

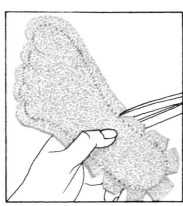

1 Cut out the basic foot shape, leaving an extra ¼in (6mm) all around the edge.

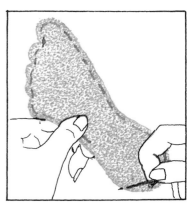

2 Snip the edge of the curved outline so that it will fold under easily.

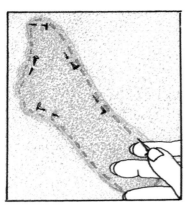

3 Tack around the edges before applying the motif. Remove these tacking stitches once the motif is in position.

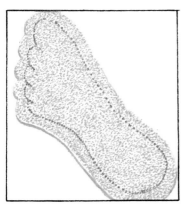

4 Pin the motif onto the base fabric and then neatly sew around the edges.

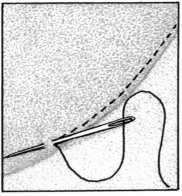

RUNNING STITCH
This is a very quick way of sewing as you can gather up several stitches in one go.

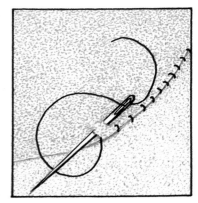

OVERSEW STITCH
If you oversew using really tiny stitches, the work is almost invisible.

A few of the many shapes that can be used in appliqué. Simple outlines are easier to work and look more distinctive than complicated ones.

Appliquéd shapes are a good way of covering up worn areas in the knees or seat of jeans. Choose geometric patches or other simple shapes with well-defined outlines, like apples, pears, bananas, moon, stars, hearts, diamonds, fish, flowers or leaves. Before sewing your shape onto the base fabric you can add more detail to it with just a few extra stitches worked either by hand or machine. For instance, if you are using a leaf motif, sew a central line in green, with two more going off from the middle to indicate veins. Add a few sequins to a star to make it shine as you walk, or give a fish a bright button for an eye.

When your shape is ready you can then pin it on the material. If you are sewing onto jeans, lay them flat and push a piece of stiff cardboard down the legs so that you do not sew right through both thicknesses of material. Pin your shape to the base material keeping everything as flat as possible. Then, sew around the shape taking each pin out as you reach it. Finish off neatly by turning the jeans inside out and oversewing a few stitches on the inside to secure the end of the thread.

Finally, press the sewn area by covering it with a piece of clean cotton cloth – sheeting will do – and ironing over it with a fairly hot iron for a minute or two.

You can get several months', if not years', more wear out of a pair of jeans by patching over the worn areas in this way.

Party drinks

Make your party different by giving your friends some really imaginative drinks – not just the usual cola or fruit squashes. There are many combinations of fruit juices and sparkling drinks as well as milk shakes that are quick to make and delicious to drink.

Some drinks are better prepared just before they are needed, particularly the ones using milk and cream. Why not let your guests help to make these? If there's a whole crowd of you in the kitchen mixing, stirring, blending and beating, everyone will soon get to know each other. So here, first of all, are a few ideas for drinks using milk, cream or ice cream. These will all serve eight people.

Minted orange cups
½ pint (300 ml) fresh orange juice
2 pints (1.2 ltrs) chilled milk
4 tablespoons whipped cream
Fresh mint leaves
Whip the orange juice and milk well together. Pour into glasses and top with whipped cream and mint leaves.

Iced coffee
1½ pints (900 ml) strong black coffee
1½ pints (900 ml) milk
8 teaspoons sugar
4 tablespoons whipped cream
Make the black coffee and add the sugar and milk. Chill. To serve, pour the mixture into eight glasses and top each with a swirl of cream.

Apple ice
1 pint (600 ml) vanilla ice cream
2 pints (1.2 ltrs) apple juice
Level teaspoon of nutmeg
4 tablespoons cream
Blend together the ice cream and apple juice until frothy. Pour into glasses. Top with a little cream and sprinkle on some nutmeg to taste.

Chocmint sizzle

6oz (150g) grated plain chocolate
4 level tablespoons fine sugar
3 pints (1.8 ltrs) milk
2 teaspoons peppermint essence
4 tablespoons whipped cream
Fresh mint leaves

Melt the chocolate and sugar in ½ pt (300 ml) milk over a low heat. Stir in the rest of the milk and peppermint essence. Take off heat, leave to cool then chill. To serve, pour the mixture into eight glasses and top with the cream and mint leaves.

SPARKLING DRINKS
Fruit punch

1 pint (600 ml) red grape juice
2 pints (1.2 ltrs) ginger ale
2 pints (1.2 ltrs) sparkling apple juice

Pour all the drinks into a large bowl or casserole dish. Cut thin slices of melon and cucumber and float them on top. Serve each glass with an ice cube or some crushed ice.

Oranges and lemons

Half-fill glasses with orange juice and top with bitter lemon. Garnish with a slice of orange or lemon.

Lemon and lime

½ pint (300 ml) lime juice cordial
3 pints (1.8 ltrs) bitter lemon
Crushed ice

Mix the lime cordial and bitter lemon together. Place some crushed ice in the bottom of each glass and pour the mixture onto it.

STILL DRINKS
Tropical taster

1 pint (600 ml) apple juice
1 pint (600 ml) lemon juice
1 pint (600 ml) orange juice
1 pint (600 ml) pineapple juice

Mix all the juices together and serve garnished with a cherry and piece of pineapple on a stick.

Blackcurrant and apple

½ pint (300 ml) blackcurrant cordial
2½ pints (1.5 ltrs) apple juice

Chill the cordial and apple juice. Mix together and serve over crushed ice for a midsummer cooler.

AND FOR COLD WINTER EVENINGS . . .
Chocmallow floats

2½ pints (1.5 ltrs) milk
4 heaped tablespoons drinking chocolate
16 marshmallows

Boil the milk, remove from heat and whip in the drinking chocolate. Pour into eight mugs and float 2 marshmallows on the top of each.

Family history

How much do you know about your family history? There may be surprising gaps in your knowledge. For instance, what is your grandmother's maiden name? How many brothers and sisters has she got? Is your grandfather an only child or one of many? Where did their parents live (your great-grandparents)? Where were they born? What jobs have people had in the past and what jobs do your present relations have? Once you start going back in time there are so many questions to ask.

Where to start?

The obvious place to start is with your own parents. They will have information about their brothers and sisters, but you will probably have to ask grandparents for information about previous generations.

Make a family tree by drawing a diagram filled with all the information you hold at present. Then you can see where the gaps are and what more information you need. Start by putting the name of your oldest known ancestor centrally at the top of a large sheet of paper, then add details of their children so that you gradually work your way down the page through the generations as shown on the opposite page. This chart has gone back only as far as grandparents and doesn't include their brothers and sisters, but already twenty-one people appear on it.

A collection of family memorabilia. Postcards, photographs and family heirlooms make our ancestors "come alive".

Grandparents will be able to provide information on their generation and their parents' families, but it may be difficult to get further back without the help of official records like birth, marriage and death certificates. County libraries often keep such details on microfiche. Once you start looking back into your family's past you will find other avenues of research. For instance, if an ancestor was a military man there are army and regimental records that might help you. There are also trade directories going back many years which would be of interest if there were family connections with trade, industry or retailing.

Some people enjoy delving into the past to see how far back they can trace their ancestors while others are more interested in the immediate family where they can actually talk to people and learn how they used to live. Often you stumble across really interesting facts that way.

Why not make a really large decorative tree chart and fill it with facts and photographs?

FAMILY TREE

Anne Smith *married* John Baker
(b. 1922) | (b. 1918)

Sarah Brown *married* Robert Green
(b. 1925) | (b. 1921)

Joan
(b. 1944)
m.
James (b. 1939)

Margaret
(b. 1946)
m.
Alec (b. 1944)

Peter   m.   Susan
(b. 1947)   (b. 1948)

Stephen
(b. 1953)
m.
Jane (b. 1958)

Jeremy   Sarah-   Simon
(b. 1974)   Anne   (b. 1979)
            (b. 1976)

Mark
(b. 1965)
m. Tanya
   (b. 1965)

Caroline   Lucy
(b. 1969)   (b. 1972)

Susanne
(b. 1986)

Elizabeth
(b. 1989)

Twenty-one people appear in this family tree, but you can take it back even further to include great-grandparents or great-aunts and great-uncles.

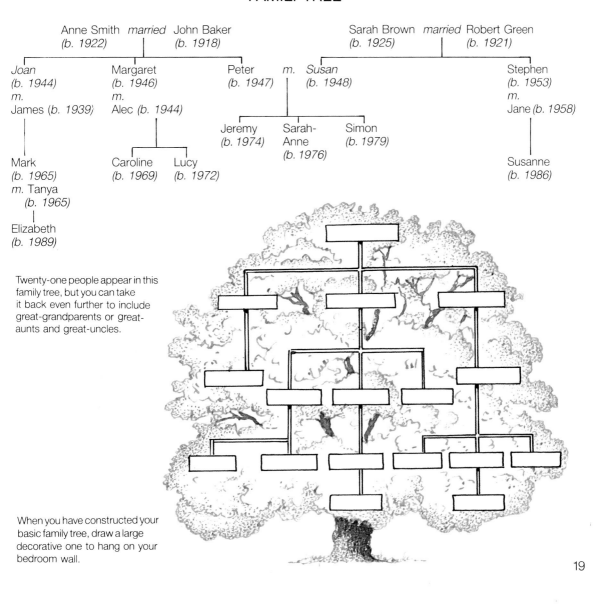

When you have constructed your basic family tree, draw a large decorative one to hang on your bedroom wall.

Flowers and herbs

Craftwork using dried herbs and flowers always makes welcome gifts and there are quite a few different items you can make.

POT POURRI

This is a mixture of dried flowers, leaves and herbs, put into open bowls or sealed in fabric to make sweet-smelling decorations. Use strong-smelling plants like lavender, thyme, rosemary, honeysuckle, roses, orange blossom, wallflowers and violets. The ingredients should be picked when quite dry and hung in a well-aired room to dry out thoroughly and naturally.

Making the mixture

When your flowers and grasses are quite dry cut off the flower heads and leaves and discard the stalks. You add spices at this stage: a pinch of nutmeg, cinnamon and cloves and some dried orange or lemon peel. The mixture can be used simply as pot pourri and left in open bowls to sweeten the air or it can be stuffed into sachets or pillows.

HERB SACHETS AND PILLOWS

Buy some cotton gingham or other material with a small flower print or look around sales for something suitable to make scented sachets. Cut out two identical shapes about 4in. (10cm) across. Sew up three sides, fill the sachet with pot pourri, close up the last side and add trimmings of ribbon and lace. Also sew on a length of ribbon for hanging the sachet onto a clothes' hanger. Two versions of the scented sachet are illustrated top right but you could also make heart, flower or leaf shapes.

Larger versions – about 12in. (30cm) across – can be used as pillows, but mix some kapok or cotton wool in with the pot pourri to make a softer cushion as dried material can be rather stiff and prickly.

An assortment of flowers and herbs should be used, chosen for their perfume and for their subtle shades.

POMANDER

A few hundred years ago a pomander was carried by fine ladies and gentlemen to keep the stench of the city streets at bay. Your bedroom hopefully hasn't such a problem, but a pomander will add a subtle spicy aroma.

First, select an unblemished orange and rub over its surface with a cloth. Tie cotton tape around the orange from top to bottom to make four segments. Now, push cloves into the fruit in neat rows in the areas between the tape, with the little "stars" resting on the skin. When the fruit is studded all over put it aside for about 6 weeks in a warm, dry place. When it has dried out, take the tape off and tie ribbons round it. Gather the ribbon ends on top and knot them into a loop so that you can hang the pomander among your clothes.

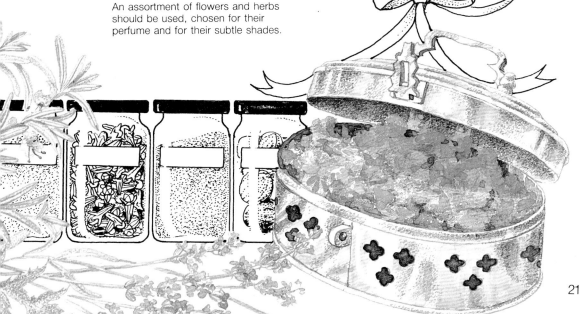

Masks

Masks can be grotesque, decorative, simple or elaborate, but always fun. The most impressive are probably the ones made from papier mâché as both depth and detail can be achieved to create stunning effects.

Other types range from simple paper bags to the highly decorated ones for fancy dress balls. Masks are often used in modern and experimental drama as they immediately change a person's appearance without using make-up, so if an actor has to portray more than one character, a mask is a quick way of effecting a personality change.

Before you make any mask, take the measurements of your face so that the eyes, nose and mouth will come in the right place. Because masks are not intended to be life-like, the holes for the eyes and mouth will be larger than is natural so they should fit other people as well.

For the papier mâché mask, first take a piece of wood or cardboard as your base and, using model clay, build up the shape of the mask. When you are satisfied you have achieved the effect you want, prepare the paste by mixing flour and water together. It needs to be about the same consistency as wallpaper paste. Tear newspaper into small strips approximately 1in (2.5cm) x 2in (5cm). Stick these all over the mask, leaving the eyes, nostrils and mouth uncovered. Apply four or five layers of paper so that you will have a really firm mask. Leave it to dry out naturally for two or three days until it feels quite hard. Then gently remove the clay from the mask. It will not come away cleanly, so make sure you scrape out all the last little pieces of clay or they will stick to your face and hair when you wear the mask. Do this carefully or you may cause damage.

You can now paint the mask with acrylic paint, or if you are using a water-based paint apply a final coat of varnish to protect it and to give it a glossy finish. Hair can be added

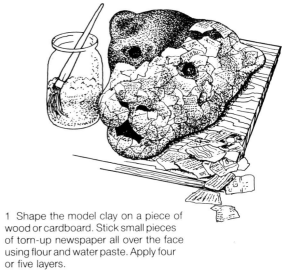

1 Shape the model clay on a piece of wood or cardboard. Stick small pieces of torn-up newspaper all over the face using flour and water paste. Apply four or five layers.

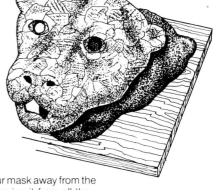

2 Gently ease your mask away from the clay, carefully removing it from all the crevices so as not to cause damage.

by sewing wool to the hair-line or by attaching wool to a piece of fabric first and then sticking that onto the mask.

Finally, make a hole either side of the mask with a darning needle and knot some elastic through the holes. Cut the elastic long enough so that it sits comfortably at the back of your head without slipping down.

HAND-HELD MASKS

These are sometimes made from papier mâché if a 3-D effect is needed, although they will not need the depth of a mask that is to be worn. The alternative is to make them from flat, stiff cardboard which is, of course, quicker and still gives scope for imaginative decoration. Attach a piece of thin dowel rod to the back of the mask with strong parcel tape. Have the rod as long as you need so that it feels comfortable to hold. If it is too short, holding it will soon make your arm ache.

For really elaborate masks, decorate with glitter, sequins, "pearl" buttons, pressed flowers, foil, gold or silver paint and anything else you can think of.

HALF-MASKS

The half-mask (bottom right) is a good one to make if you are taking part in a carnival procession as it allows you to keep both hands free to help you to keep your balance. (Remember those times when you were holding a banner with one hand and clutching on to your hat with the other, while balancing

precariously on a farm trailer with increasingly wobbly legs?)

Again, this mask can be made from thin cardboard with elastic attached to the sides.

Hand-held masks made from papier mâché and cardboard.

Right Half-masks are a good disguise and completely change a person's appearance.

Left A paper bag, scissors, sticky tape and felt-tip pens are all you need to make this mask.

23

Fun with dyes

There are so many ways of dyeing fabric that it's great fun planning to give your old clothes a new lease of life. You can even dye small items in a microwave! Most fabrics can be dyed successfully, but the manufacturer's instructions on the dyes will give you detailed information.

Cotton T-shirts make particularly good subjects. Try "the scrunch", tie and dye, or pleating to revitalize a much-worn shirt. If you want to use the microwave method you will need a small packet of natural fabric dye, a microwave oven (of course), a bowl suitable for putting in a microwave, a polythene bag, rubber gloves, plastic spoon and the amount of water recommended. Do not use a microwave for any garments that have metal zippers, buttons or studs.

Make up the dye in the bowl, as directed, stirring with the plastic spoon. Put the garment into the bowl, scrunched, tied or pleated, cover the bowl with a polythene bag and then put it into the microwave, setting it on high for four minutes. Then, at the end of the four minutes, using an oven cloth or glove, remove the bowl from the oven. Tip the dye away and rinse the garment in cold water before undoing any ties. Keep changing the rinsing water until the water remains clear or almost clear. Then wash the garment with washing powder and hot water to remove any remaining dye.

If you want a subtle shaded effect, wash your garment first and leave it damp before dyeing. For a bolder effect, make sure the fabric is clean and dry.

With fabric-dye paints and pens you can add freehand decoration to T-shirts, jeans and

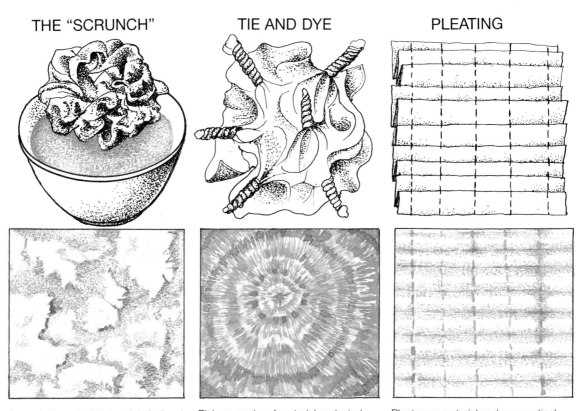

THE "SCRUNCH"	TIE AND DYE	PLEATING

Scrunch the material into a tight ball and immerse it in a small bowl containing the dye for a random effect.

Pick up peaks of material and wind thread tightly around to a depth of about 3in (7.5cm). This produces a web-like effect.

Pleat your material and sew vertical lines of thread through the pleats to hold it in position while it is being dyed. This gives a more regular pattern of vertical and horizontal lines.

canvas shoes. Copy a design, pattern or illustration onto your T-shirt in outline, then fill in the solid areas.

For an informal look, why not try scribbling, spattering or splashing? An even scribble, or perhaps some doodles, drawn all over your tattered jeans, will give them an "interesting" look. For the "spattered" look, you need some fabric paint, a nail brush and a flat object, like a ruler. You must also put a protective cover over everything within spattering distance, including yourself. Spread your garment out flat, then dip the brush in the paint, aim it at the fabric and draw the ruler across it from front to back. This will make the paint spatter over the surface of the T-shirt or whatever you are decorating and give it the appearance of used blotting paper.

The splashing technique is very similar. Again, you must cover all surfaces in the immediate area. Then, using a large paint brush, dip it into the paint and "throw" the paint at the fabric. Do this all over the front of the garment, wait for it to dry, then use the same technique on the back. When the whole garment is dry, place a clean cloth on it and iron over the whole surface for a few minutes to make your design permanent.

The effect becomes even more dramatic when you spatter paint onto pre-printed fabric. Try red or yellow on a black T-shirt or ski pants, orange or white on brown, and purple or emerald green on a really dark blue.

Handprints or fingerprints are also fun or why not stencil a design on? You can buy pre-cut stencils, but it's easy to make your own using thin cardboard. Keep your design simple so that it's easy to cut out. Also, the clearer the outline is, the more effective the stencil will look.

Attach the stencil to your T-shirt with sticky tape so that it does not move when you begin work. You can use a hard-bristled stencil brush or a thick pad of sheeting material for applying the dye. Remember to put a piece of cardboard inside your T-shirt before you start or the dye will seep through to the back as well.

Dramatic effects can be produced with fabric dyes that are used like paint. Ironing over the design makes it permanent.

Painting patterns on canvas shoes is great fun, but plan out your design before you start to achieve a really professional look.

Studying wildlife

When you take a walk outside your home just see how many small creatures and insects you can find by looking carefully in the bushes, behind leaves and under stones. Keep watch, too, from inside to see what birds and butterflies are around when no one is about.

BUTTERFLIES

The butterfly population has decreased because chemical sprays have destroyed many of their traditional food sources, such as wild flowers and nettles. They lay their eggs on plant leaves and when the caterpillars hatch out they then feed on the plant. This is not always good news for the gardener as a host of caterpillars can strip a fruit bush in a very short time indeed. When fully grown, the caterpillar turns into a pupa or chrysalis from which the butterfly or moth gradually emerges.

To study this process, find a caterpillar and put it in a jar with some leaves from the plant on which you found it. Drop in a few twigs as well so that the caterpillar has something to climb on. Add fresh leaves daily and clear out the droppings regularly. As the caterpillar grows and becomes too big for its skin, it will shed it and grow another one. Keep the jar out of direct sunlight.

When the caterpillar changes into a pupa, keep a close watch on it so that when the butterfly or moth emerges you can set it free. Depending on the species, this process can take weeks or months.

BEETLES

You can do a survey of beetles by sinking a glass jar into the earth. Make a hole just big enough for the jar to sit in so that the rim is level with the surrounding earth.

An insect trap

Put a few scraps of food in the bottom to attract beetles to crawl in. Cover the jar with a tile or piece of wood, supported on two bricks, to keep the rain out.

Look into your jar each morning and note what has fallen in overnight. Obviously you will then let your captives go.

BEES

You may be lucky enough to find a wild bees' nest near your house. It may be in a tree or in the ground but take care not to disturb it. The worker bees collect pollen and nectar from the flowers and turn it into honey. They also keep the hive clean, feed the queen bee and the larvae. Some workers guard the hive and keep it cool by fanning it with their wings.

WORMS

If you want to study worms successfully why not make a wormery? The only materials you will have to buy are 2 pieces of wood 8in x 1in (20cm x 2.5cm), 1 piece of wood 12in x 1in (30cm x 2.5cm), 2 pieces of clear acrylic sheet 8in x 12in (20cm x 30cm), some screws and a tube of glue.

Glue the wood together to make a frame and screw the acrylic sheet onto each side of the frame. Put in 3 or 4 layers of different soils (perhaps chalk, sand, peat or earth) so you will be able to see how the worms mix up the soils. They do a useful job of work in aerating the soil as well as turning it over. Put a variety of different leaves on top of the soil and see if the worms prefer any particular kind.

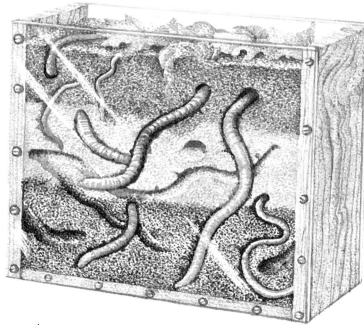

A wormery showing how the worms enrich the soil by pulling down vegetable matter and aerating the ground.

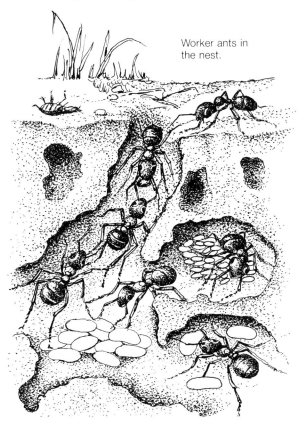

Worker ants in the nest.

The best time to find worms is either on warm, damp evenings or early in the morning Put the wormery in a dark cool place and keep the soil moist. Let the worms go when you have finished studying them.

ANTS

Ants are more difficult to study as most of their activities take place underground where they live in colonies. All the eggs are laid by the queen ant, and there are, at the most, two of these per colony. The eggs hatch into larvae (or grubs) which are fed by the queen and eventually turn into pupae.

Ants eat both plant and animal material and will carry seeds and dead insects back to the nest. They also like decaying fruit and are particularly partial to sweet things. If you leave a saucer of jam, syrup or fruit juice outside, away from the house, you will notice that the ants soon find it and there will be a steady stream of them from the nest to the saucer and back again.

Mobiles

To make a successful mobile all you have to remember is that it needs shape, balance and movement to function properly.

Shape

Decide upon the subject: perhaps things that really fly, like birds or butterflies, planes, space probes or hot air balloons, or things that swim, like fish, whales or seals. Alternatively you may prefer something totally incongruous like flying fruit.

Whatever you choose should be bright and striking with the pattern on both sides of the cut-out. Or use foil as an alternative to paint to give a shiny surface to catch the light and work some sequins into your design to add sparkle.

Balance

Find out how the different pieces balance by attaching strong thread to the top of each piece and then holding it up to make sure that it will hang the way that you want it to. All of the butterflies on this page are symmetrical and hang upright, but if you had a flock of vampire bats you might want some swooping and others soaring. Next lay the threaded pieces on a table and arrange all of them in such a way that they make a pleasing overall shape. Avoid, as far as possible, putting two large shapes side by side as they may well bump into each other as they turn around. Then lay your supporting rods in position. These can either be

Above and right
These fruit and bird mobiles make use of coat hangers as their main support.

28

thin wooden dowel rods or metal rods, like bicycle spokes. Tie the thread to the rods and it is ready to be hung in position.

Movement
Spend a little while deciding where to hang your mobile. If it is to go in your room you will probably want to see it from the bed, but will not want it where it might be in the way – for instance, just inside the door. Neither should you put it where a sudden gust of air (as from an open window) will catch it and tangle the thread. The best position is where you will see it against a plain background and if it can be placed above a radiator, it will turn constantly all winter in the rising currents of warm air.

Hanging the mobile
To make your mobile hang evenly, without the shapes colliding with each other, it may be necessary to move the thread along the rods and to shorten or lengthen some pieces.

Ideally, try to get the mobile to "turn within itself" so that all these butterflies, for instance, can turn past each other on different levels without ever touching. As it can take a little while to adjust the lengths of thread and their position on the rods, it is a good idea to hang the mobile where you can fiddle with it in comfort rather than standing on a chair and getting aching arms.

Collecting

Apart from stamps, mentioned on pages 38 and 39, there are many other things that are very collectable.

PICTURE CARDS

Grandparents probably collected cigarette cards rather than stamps as they were more readily available. Many companies included a card in their cigarette packets and the aim was to collect a complete set. It might be ships, famous actors, historical figures or a host of other subjects. There are still avid collectors of old cigarette cards, and you can often find incomplete sets or odd cards at flea markets, rummage sales and dark corners of antique shops, so this is a good hobby for the collector who likes rummaging around.

FREEBIES

If you find you are always short of cash, then start collecting freebies. These are the multitude of things given away with comics, for instance, or magazines and packaged foods, particularly breakfast cereals. It may be a small plastic toy, a picture card, a hologram or a badge. When you have the complete set, mount it on cardboard for display in your room. There are always new and different freebies coming along as manufacturers search for a fresh gimmick that will entice customers to buy their product, so this forms an interesting, on-going collection that costs

This illustration shows a varied selection of items that have proved popular with collectors.

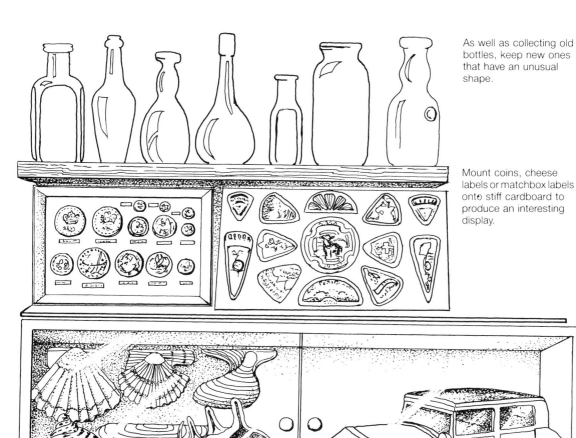

As well as collecting old bottles, keep new ones that have an unusual shape.

Mount coins, cheese labels or matchbox labels onto stiff cardboard to produce an interesting display.

nothing, providing you don't mind eating your way through packets of honey-coated, sugar-frosted crunchy-munchy cereals!

COINS

If you often travel to other countries, why not start a coin collection – just keep one example of each value. You can build on this by adding old coins. Your own family may have some coins that are now out of circulation, but you can add to these by visiting coin fairs where both common and rare examples are bought and sold.

If you have an opportunity to visit a collectors' fair, do go as you will be amazed at the odd and unusual things people do collect, and it may give you other ideas, too.

DISPLAYING YOUR COLLECTION

Once you have a reasonably-sized collection, then work out how to display it to best advantage. Some things, like model cars or shells, that are difficult to dust, would be better in a glass case, but a bottle collection or anything mounted on cardboard could be displayed on open shelves.

A simple shelf made from a plank of wood and two brackets will support most things except perhaps the heaviest rock samples in a geological collection. An old bookcase, brightly painted, can also serve as a useful display area. Have a look in local museums and the windows of large stores to get some ideas on the best way to group, display and label your collection.

Block printing

Use a small knife when making your
potato block as it is easier to control.
A fruit knife is ideal.

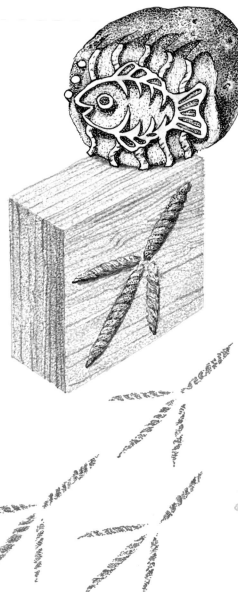

Block printing is just what it says it is –
printing using a block of some sort. In this
case it is a potato block and string glued onto
a wooden block. Poster paints can be used.
You will soon find out how much paint you
need to have on your block to make a good
print – too much and the print will be very
blobby, too little and parts of the print may
not come out.

POTATO PRINTS

You may have regarded potato prints as kids'
stuff *until now.* But amazingly sophisticated
designs can be produced as potatoes are very
easy to carve.

Using the potato block, you could print a
frieze around the wall of your room. Or you
could brighten up your science folder with
prints of test tubes, flasks and bunsen
burners, and your history folder with shields,
swords and helmets.

STRING PRINTS

The list of materials for string prints is very
short: 1) a block of wood 2) some string 3)
some glue. The instructions are equally brief.
Draw out a simple design on paper. Cover the
block of wood with glue and press the string
onto the wood in the shape you have chosen.
Remember, prints always reverse so if you
want to print a tortoise facing left you will
have to make it face right on the block.

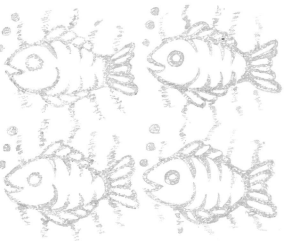

Make the shapes as simple as possible.
Complicated detail will not show up on
the print.

PRINTING ON CLOTHES

Why not use potato prints to personalize a T-shirt? Cut your initials on two halves of a potato and print them around the neck, then make a circular pattern in the middle of the shirt for a totally unique garment.

If you are printing on a T-shirt or jeans you will need to use a permanent dye specially made for fabric painting. The household department of your nearest large store should stock them. The technique for using these dyes is very simple.

First of all, lay down lots of newspaper, just in case of accidents. Then secure your T-shirt or whatever to a board with sticky tape so that the garment is flat but not overstretched as this will distort your pattern. Slip a piece of thin cardboard inside so that the dye does not go through to the back of the shirt.

Pour a little of the dye into a saucer, dip the potato in it, shake off any excess and press the potato down firmly onto the fabric. When your pattern is complete, leave it to dry, then cover it with a clean cotton cloth and iron all over the dyed area with a very hot iron for 1-2 minutes, keeping the iron moving all the time. This will make your design permanent.

You can make some very striking string-print designs using these dyes. Make two different blocks and print a random design all over the T-shirt, or on the sleeves only. Have a patterned area straight down the front or diagonally from shoulder to hip. Use a string circle and a cross to print a game with noughts and crosses – tic tac toe!

The possibilities for designs made in this way are endless. You can make co-ordinating or matching scarves, ties and belts as well as liven up some of your older clothes with a bold new pattern.

Use a combination of blocks to produce more intricate patterns and designs.

Quick snacks

Here are a few ways of preparing some quick snack meals that you can try out when you want to make your own supper, or when friends drop in unexpectedly.

Several of these "Five-minute wonders" are based on bread, but filled pancakes are also quick to make and there's a very crafty way of making spaghetti bolognese which may not taste exactly like the real thing, but is a good substitute.

TOASTED SANDWICHES

The most basic toasted sandwich you can get is a cheese one. Simply make a cheese sandwich, and toast both sides. What could be easier?

Variations

Cheese and tomato; cheese and ham; cheese and apple; cheese and pickle; cheese and onion.

OPEN SANDWICHES

If you prefer your sandwiches open, then toast one side of the bread only, butter the other side, lay on your "filling" and then re-heat for a few minutes.

"Fillings"

1 Cheese with tomato on top
2 Baked beans with cheese on top
3 Tomato purée topped with cheese and garlic sausage
4 Ham, cheese and a pineapple ring

THINGS ON TOAST

Scrambled egg is a good "thing" to have on toast as there are so many other foods you can add to it to give some variety.

The basic mixture is made from a beaten egg with a little milk added plus salt and pepper to taste. Melt a knob of butter or margarine in a saucepan until it just begins to bubble, then add the beaten egg and stir until it becomes firm. You can add cheese to it at this stage or tomato, mushrooms or herbs. Alternatively you could fry some bacon or onion and then add the egg to it, stirring the mixture until it is completely cooked.

Baked beans can also come in several disguises.
1 Topped with grated cheese.
2 With curry powder added.
3 Mixed with a couple of frankfurters.

EGGY BREAD

Beat an egg with a little salt and pepper and dip a slice of bread into the mixture. Heat some butter or oil in a shallow pan and fry both sides of the bread. Or, cut a circle in a slice of bread. Place the bread in a pan and crack an egg in the hole. When one side is done, turn the whole thing over and fry the other side as well.

PANCAKES

Ingredients

4 oz (100g) flour	½ pint (250ml) milk
Pinch salt	Cooking oil
1 egg	

Method

Sift the flour and salt into a bowl. Break the egg into the flour and mix well. Gradually add half the milk, stirring the mixture all the time, then beat it to a smooth batter. Stir in the rest of the milk.

Heat 1 tablespoon of oil in a shallow, non-stick pan. When it is hot, pour in 3 tablespoonsful of the batter or more if you like larger pancakes. Cook for a minute or two until it is golden brown then turn over with a fish slice or spatula and cook the other side for about the same length of time. Cook the remaining pancakes and keep warm.

Fillings

1 Grilled or fried bacon with fried onions.
2 Any left-over sauces e.g. bolognese, chicken in white sauce, mushrooms and cashews in white sauce, curry sauce.
3 Mix a small can of tuna with 4 tablespoons natural yoghurt, fill the pancakes, roll up and place in greased heatproof dish. Sprinkle with grated cheese and pop in a preheated oven (180°C, 350°F, Gas No 4) for 20 minutes.

QUICK SPAGHETTI BOLOGNESE

14oz (400g) can spaghetti
7¾oz (220g) can minced meat
Level teaspoon garlic powder
Level teaspoon mixed herbs
A few shakes of pepper
Grated cheese

In a saucepan, mix together spaghetti, meat, garlic powder, herbs and pepper and heat until mixture begins to bubble. Turn into a heatproof dish, sprinkle with grated cheese and pop in a warm oven until the cheese has melted. Eat at once.

Pressed flowers

Have you ever tried pressing flowers? It's really quite simple and if you have an eye for design when it comes to making up a picture or a greetings card, so much the better. There are lots of books published on the subject so spend some time looking through a few in your local library and you will soon have plenty of ideas. The more designs you make, the better you will become.

Flowers can be pressed between the leaves of large books – old telephone directories are particularly good as their pages are absorbent and it won't matter if you spoil them.

Remember to place your flower in absorbent kitchen paper before using the press *(below)*.

HOW TO PRESS

Flowers or leaves should be picked when they are quite dry. If they are very "fleshy", like tulips or roses, you will have to press individual petals, but more delicate flowers such as buttercups, daisies or poppies can be pressed whole.

Lay your flowers between sheets of absorbent paper and make sure they lie flat in the book. Turn over about twelve pages before putting the next batch in to press and so on through the book.

Weight the book down with bricks or more directories and leave for about four weeks.

Making a flower press

If you haven't the space to leave large directories and bricks lying around, you can try making a proper flower press.

You need two pieces of wood ¾ in. (2cm) thick and any size you wish to make it. A small one could be 6 in. (15cm) square or a larger one could be as much as 12 in. (30cm) square.

Buy 4 bolts 4 in. x ⅜ in. (10cm x 9mm) with washers and butterfly screws and ask someone to drill ⅜ in. (9mm) holes in all four corners of both pieces of wood. You will also need several sheets of cardboard to sit between each layer. Place flowers in absorbent paper, as before, and insert between the layers of cardboard.

Turn butterfly screws as tightly as possible and leave for about four weeks.

PRESSED FLOWER PICTURES

Framed pictures of pressed flowers make attractive presents
as well as being good fund-raisers. Arrange your flowers and
leaves to display them to best advantage. Choose a tinted
paper to stick them on: bright flowers look good on pale
cream, green or blue paper while white, cream or yellow
flowers look better on a darker shade.

CARDS AND BOOKMARKS

Cards are another obvious way of using pressed flowers.
Again, as with the pictures, use a tinted, fairly stiff cardboard.
You could attach the flowers to the front or cut out an oval
to reveal the flowers on the inside.

   Professionally-made pressed flower cards cost quite a lot
so this is another good money-spinning idea for raising funds
for a special charity or your local youth group.

   For bookmarks, choose tiny flowers like forget-me-nots,
buttercups or daisies, or why not use just leaves for a different
effect? – ones collected when they are turning yellow, orange
and brown look particularly attractive.

   You will need to cover the bookmark with adhesive
transparent film which can be bought from most stationers.
Cut a piece large enough to wrap right around to the back,
and trim off any excess.

Stamp collecting

You may already have started a small collection of stamps. Most of us go through the stamp collecting fad when we are quite young and some people develop it into an absorbing pastime right through life. Some collectors concentrate on a certain subject like transport, birds, butterflies, animals or sport while others may devote their collection to just a few countries.

Joining a stamp club, either local or national, will keep you up-to-date with all the news from the stamp world as well as introducing you to bargain offers, so it's well worth becoming a member.

How to start

Begin by buying a stamp album, a large packet of assorted stamps and some hinges. Choose a stamp album that has notes on identifying stamps as not all of them will be immediately recognizable. For instance, stamps with Magyar on them are Hungarian and those that have the word Helvetia on them are from Switzerland.

Mounting the stamps

When you have sorted your stamps out into individual countries you can put them in your album. Always attach your stamps to the page using stamp hinges so that if you wish to swop the one in the album for a better specimen, it will be easy to remove. Never glue stamps down as this diminishes any value they might have and you may one day come across a rare or valuable one.

Fold the stamp hinge in half with the sticky side facing outwards and gently moisten it. If you wet it too much you may find that it won't stick. Then attach the folded hinge to the back of the stamp and press it down firmly on the page.

Soaking stamps

Once friends and relatives know you collect stamps they will begin to save them for you. This way you will get stamps from all over the world. You'll have to soak them off the envelope unless this has already been done for you.

Place the stamps in a bowl of lukewarm (not hot) water for about ten minutes. At the end of this time the stamp should easily peel away from the envelope. If not, pop it back in the water for another few minutes. Have some clean blotting paper ready and lay the stamp on this, face down. Allow the stamp to dry out completely before you mount it in your album.

Other equipment
The only other equipment you might consider buying is a pair of tweezers, if you find mounting stamps a fiddly business, and a magnifying glass. Sometimes the country of origin is partially obscured by the postmark so a magnifying glass would help you identify the country of origin. Also the detail on some stamps is so fine that it can only be appreciated with the aid of a magnifying glass. They can be bought at most stores that sell stationery.

Specializing
When you've been collecting stamps for a while you may feel you also wish to start a specialist collection. This could mean choosing to collect stamps just from certain countries or stamps on certain themes, like famous people, natural history, flight or any of the themes mentioned on the previous page.

Duplicates
If you start by buying assorted packets of stamps you may find you end up with duplicates of particular ones. Ask around among your friends and see if anyone else collects stamps then you could perhaps swop your duplicates for other stamps that you haven't got. If your school hasn't got a stamp club perhaps a few of you could start one where you could swop the latest stamp news as well as duplicates.

Soaking stamps off envelopes is a simple operation. You need just a flat dish, some warm water and a sheet of absorbent paper.

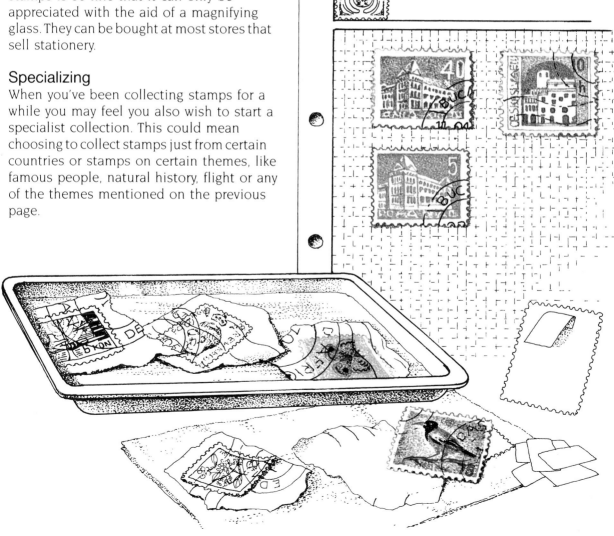

Paper hang-ups

Paper hang-ups are really just fun things; they don't actually "do" anything, but they're something to make on a wet afternoon. Hang-ups are, in fact, immensely popular and shops and stores specializing in wrapping paper or papercraft things sell inflatable ones in large numbers.

But you can easily make them out of paper. They are simplicity itself. Start with a small one to get the shape and proportion right and then you can go on to make larger than life examples.

MAKING A HANG-UP

The two hang-ups on this page are made in the same way. Select a piece of fairly stiff paper and fold it in half. Draw half the shape on the folded edge, as shown in the illustration on the right, then cut round it through both thicknesses.

The Bird

Draw in the detail of wings, eyes, beak etc., then suspend it from the ceiling using button thread which is strong but not too noticeable. You can hang it from two threads attached along the fold-line of the body or from the wing tips. If you attach it to the wings, stick a small piece of card between the wings just behind the head of the bird and this will help to prevent the wings from folding up and will give you a better illusion of flight.

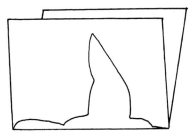

For the bird and jabberwock, fold the paper in half, draw on one side only and cut through both thicknesses.

The jabberwock

For a really spectacular hang-up, try the jabberwock from "Alice Through the Looking Glass". A flock of these flying around your room would certainly look different!

The same principle applies when cutting out, except the head is drawn separately and then stuck on to the neck so that it can peer at friends and nervous relatives. After you have cut out the body, bend the head and legs down and the wings and tails up, then stick the head onto the neck. Suspend the jabberwock by button thread sewn through the wing tips and middle of the tail. Try a really big one, say 4ft (1.3m) long. In "Alice" the jabberwock was said to have "eyes of flame" which could be painted on or made out of red, shiny paper.

Flat hang-ups

The pig is made from a flat piece of stiff pink paper. Draw the outline and fill in as much detail as you want. Maybe even give it foil "spots" to catch the light as it moves on its thread. Cut out two wings allowing an extra 1in (2.5cm) at the base of each wing. Cut a slot in the side of the pig. Push one wing tip through this and glue it to the other wing. To make it reallly secure, bind some sticky tape around the join. Suspend the pig from two pieces of thread attached to the wings.

You can make lots of different flat hang-ups using this method; try some small ones as well as larger ones, like the pig here. Have a sparkling moon and stars in one corner of your room. Cover them all over with gold, silver and blue glitter and watch how they catch the light.

Keeping a scrapbook

When you read something in a newspaper or magazine that you want to keep, why not cut it out and keep it in a scrapbook? That way, you'll have no trouble finding the clipping when you need it.

You'll also be able to build up your own reference library for subjects that interest you. So will just one scrapbook do, or do you need one for each hobby or interest? Motor racing, for instance, football or fashion, recipes or pop stars.

How to start

First of all, buy a scrapbook. Keep all your clippings in a large envelope so that you can sort them out at leisure, then stick the envelope to the inside cover of your

A scrapbook of UFOs (Unidentified Flying Objects) will contain newspaper and magazine articles and cartoons, as well as your own reports of broadcasts and television programmes.

scrapbook. Any future clippings can be popped inside, then, when you have some free time, you can spend a while arranging them so that the pages are pleasing to look at.

There is no point in rushing out to buy four scrapbooks only to find that in six months of looking, you've found only one article for the scrapbook devoted to that most popular of animals, the aardvark. But when you find you have enough material for another scrapbook, then go out and buy one.

You will no doubt also need a "General Purpose" scrapbook for all those worthwhile odds and ends that otherwise have nowhere to go and may end up in a crumpled heap somewhere. This is a useful scrapbook to have as you can include all those strange and amazing things that happen around the world, as well as humorous articles and jokes that you have heard from friends or radio or TV.

Choosing a scrapbook

Do keep things orderly as they are so much easier to find. The traditional scrapbook may not be quite right for your needs, particularly if you intend keeping clippings in alphabetical or chronological (time) order. In these cases you might need to insert extra pages, in which case a loose-leaf notebook would be better where you could increase the number of pages when necessary. If you intend keeping things like bus or concert tickets, then a loose-leaf photograph album might be the answer as the see-through adhesive flaps would keep everything in place.

Design

Keep an eye on the overall design of the pages. It is better to pop clippings in an envelope and set aside an evening or weekend afternoon for laying out your pages and sticking the clippings in.

If you look at the illustration here you can see that a spread that is not overfull looks pleasing and easy to read. But in other cases a montage of pictures or cartoons is very effective. Spend some time working out the best way of arranging your material and don't forget to write short captions with dates so that, when you come to read an article months or even years later, you'll know when it was written.

A varied selection of clippings awaiting inclusion in individual subject scrapbooks. Keep them flat until you have time to sort through them.

Papier mâché sculpture

Papier mâché is often used for masks, money-boxes, puppets and beads, but it can also be used to make light-weight and imaginative sculptures. All the basic materials should be readily to hand, but you may have to buy some wire if you intend building your sculpture onto a wire base.

For papier mâché work you need lots of newspaper, paste made from flour and water, an old paint brush, petroleum jelly, acrylic paints, or if you are using a non-glossy paint apply a final coat of varnish.

Method

1 Tear up strips of newspaper 1in (2.5cm) x 2in (5cm) long. Be sure to have a large pile of strips then you won't have to stop halfway through to tear off more.

2 Mix the flour and water paste so that it is quite thick, but can easily be stirred – similar to the consistency of wallpaper paste.

3 Choose something to use as your basic shape, like the old boot pictured below, and grease it all over with petroleum jelly.

4 Paste the strips on so that they overlap each other and eventually cover the boot completely. For a really firm result, apply eight or nine layers.

5 Leave to dry out completely and it will harden as it dries. You can smooth down the surface with fine glasspaper.

6 Using a craft knife, cut carefully around the boot to divide it into two halves so that you can easily remove it. Join the two halves from the inside with sticky tape, then glue some more strips of paper over the join, both to strengthen it and to hide the cut marks.

7 When the finished boot is completely dry, smooth off any rough edges with glasspaper, then apply at least two coats of paint for an even finish.

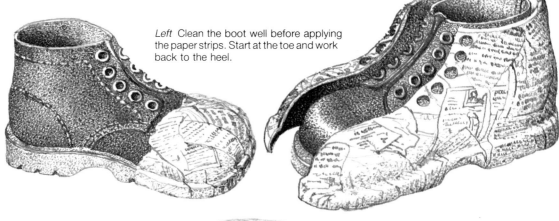

Left Clean the boot well before applying the paper strips. Start at the toe and work back to the heel.

Above Cut the papier mâché in half lengthways and ease it gently off the boot.

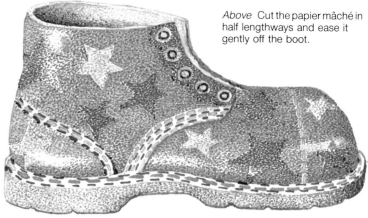

Right A completed piece of modern sculpture that would deserve a place in an art gallery! You could give it a surreal look by painting sky and clouds or a landscape all over it.

To make the figure like the one illustrated here, you will need some strong wire and soft model clay as well as the usual materials for making papier mâché. Use a small block of wood for your base, then start to model the outline of your figure in wire. Add small amounts of model clay to those parts of the body where a little fullness is required: feet, knees, hands, hips, elbows, shoulders and head. When you are satisfied that.you have the shape roughly as you want it, secure it to the wooden base with two heavy duty staples, used for fixing wire to walls.

If you want it to look reasonably life-like, copy the proportions from a photograph so that the arms aren't too long or the head too small. For example, the head is calculated to be about one-seventh the length of the whole body.

You may, though, choose to do a "stretched" figure, giving it a gaunt appearance, rather like a Giacometti sculpture. In this case, arms, legs and body are extended to make a long, thin outline.

Now cover the whole statue with a layer of papier mâché, as described on the previous page, adding more layers until you have the shape you want. When it is dry, paint it silver or gold for a metallic look or leave it unpainted but add a coat of varnish for a glossy finish.

Make the outline skeleton first then prepare a bowl of flour and water paste. Tear the newspaper into strips as the rough edges are easier to smooth down than neat ones cut with scissors.

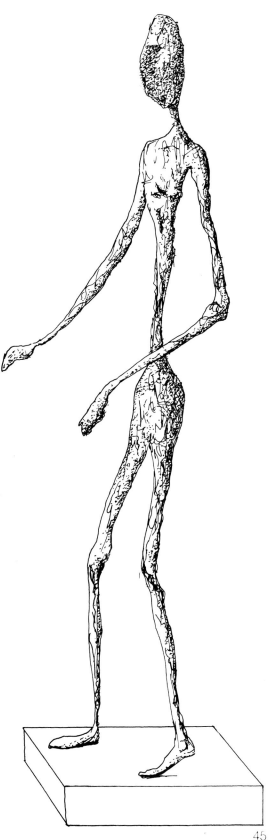

Ponds

If you have a pond you will find it attracts a host of creatures which are totally dependent on water for their existence. Ponds take a little while to establish themselves but soon support a great variety of wildlife. Even if you have room for only a very small one it is better than nothing at all. Try not to site it directly under a tree or you will have problems when the leaves fall.

Select a fairly sunny position for your pond and dig a hole, with sloping sides, that is no more than 18in (45cm) deep at its deepest point. It is essential that there is a gradual deepening of the pond to allow any small animals that may fall in to crawl out again.

You should keep any grass turves as these will be needed to edge the finished pond and the earth that is removed can form a bank on one side of it.

Lining and filling the pond

You will need to buy a large sheet of heavy-duty polythene for lining the pond. This can be obtained from most stores specializing in gardening equipment. Buy it big enough to extend well beyond the edge of the pond. When you have finished digging, press down the soil in the hole and remove any large or sharp stones or other debris that might puncture the polythene.

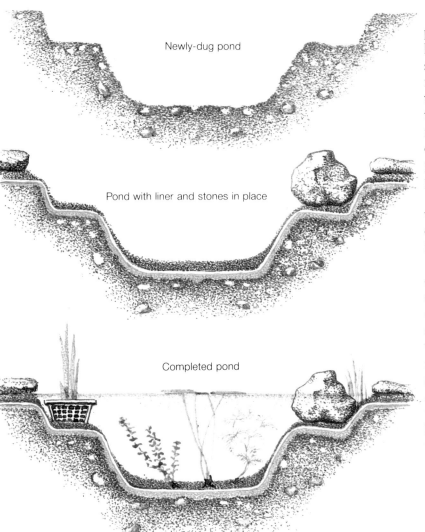

Newly-dug pond

Pond with liner and stones in place

Completed pond

Before putting the polythene in place, line the hole with either damp sand or several thicknesses of newspaper. Then spread out the liner carefully and secure the edges with large stones making sure the liner is slack enough to fit the shape of the pond once the water is poured in.

Now fill the pond with water and wait two or three days for the liner to settle. Leaving an overlap of at least 10in (25cm), trim off any excess lining. Put back the earth and turves around the edge of the pond and arrange a few large flat stones there as well. Scatter some fine earth into the pond so plants can grow there and if you can find a large enough stone place this at the shallow end for birds, and hopefully frogs, to use as an island.

Pond plants

These are necessary for oxygenating the water and using up the carbon dioxide which will be produced by the creatures that live in it.

The three types you should aim to buy are ones that float on the surface, oxygenators that are unseen but do vital work at the bottom of ponds and then plants that grow in the shallows. You can find all these in a natural pond but buying them from a specialist dealer ensures they will be pest- and disease-free. You may find it easier to submerge plants in containers then they can easily be removed or changed.

Pond creatures

Although you will find that many creatures will magically find their way to your pond under their own steam, it is worth introducing one or two to begin with. Water snails will help to clear up the rubbish that accumulates in any pond and will also eat the algae that will inevitably appear. You could also add beetles, water spiders and frog and toad spawn in the spring. Other insects, like water boatmen, pond skaters and dragonflies, will find their own way to your pond. Birds of course will use it for drinking water and may even bathe in the shallows, and will also be attracted by the ever-present food supply of gnats and midges during the summer months. It is better not to have fish in a small pond as sticklebacks and minnows will make a meal of the other pond creatures and goldfish, who feed on the bottom of ponds, stir the mud up and so cloud the water.

Ponds with a well-balanced population need very little care. Make sure the water level is maintained and remove fallen leaves. Apart from that, it will look after itself.

Decorative ties and belts

Ties and belts, decorated in new and unusual ways, make really good fashion extras.

Basic, plain cotton ties are not expensive to buy and can be customized in many different ways for everyday or partytime wear.

Use fabric dyes in the form of paints and pens as your medium and look back to the sections on dyeing and block printing to see the different ways in which these can be used.

Try to work out a design that takes into account the shape of the tie. A giraffe, for instance, would be a suitable outline to fit within the area of the tie, but an elephant, of course, would not.

Draw a tall shape, like the Eiffel Tower or the leaning tower of Pisa, onto a blue tie and add a few fluffy white clouds in the background. Using a nailbrush, ruler and

fabric paints (as described on pages 24 and 25), splatter a shower of white snowflakes onto a silver tie and paint a snowman or giant snowflake at the bottom. Paint bright red toadstools onto a buttercup-yellow tie for a startling effect or cover the whole tie with a tropical jungle. For a more subtle look, try block printing with potatoes or string blocks as described on pages 32 and 33.

For parties, a dramatic effect can be achieved by sewing gold or silver sequins onto a dark blue or black background. Stitch them on fairly thickly just below the knot, but space them out down the length of the tie to give a shower-like appearance.

Bow ties can be made from two pieces of material, placed one behind the other, with a narrower strip of the same material stitched around the middle pulling the fabric in to achieve the bow effect. Attach the bow to your shirt with a safety pin or use a length of elastic that will be hidden under the collar.

Easy-to-make bow ties add style to a shirt or blouse.

A selection of ties, decorated in a variety of ways, will give the same outfit a different look each time you wear it.

Linked belt

Leather is the best material to use for this belt, although a strong fabric could be used; it would be advisable to use a double thickness stuck together with a fabric glue. Cut out several elongated figures of eight from strips of material 5in (12.5cm) long by 2in (5cm) wide. The easiest way of doing this is to fold the material in half and cut an egg-shaped hole in the middle, then trim the edge of the fabric to give it a rounded shape, making sure you do not cut the material right through at the folded edge. Thread each link through the preceding one as shown until you have enough to go around your waist. The belt can be fastened with leather thongs tied to the two end links.

Braided belt

You will need ten or twelve lengths of assorted braids at least 5ft (1.5m) long. Knot both ends of each length of braid to prevent them fraying. For a more decorative look, thread a bead onto each end and then tie the knot.

To make all these separate strands into a belt you will have to wind a thinner braid around them all at 6in (15cm) intervals. Twist all the braids slightly before you bind them together to give a tighter look to your belt. You could use silver or gold thread as an alternative to the thinner braid, and you will need about 18in (45cm) lengths to bind the belt adequately.

Leather belts

Leather is a useful material for belts as it is sturdy and keeps its shape and if you buy the soft kind it is also easy to work with. Because it does not easily tear a plain leather belt can be fastened with thongs threaded through holes punched into each end. Decorate with appliquéd shapes or printed or stencilled designs.

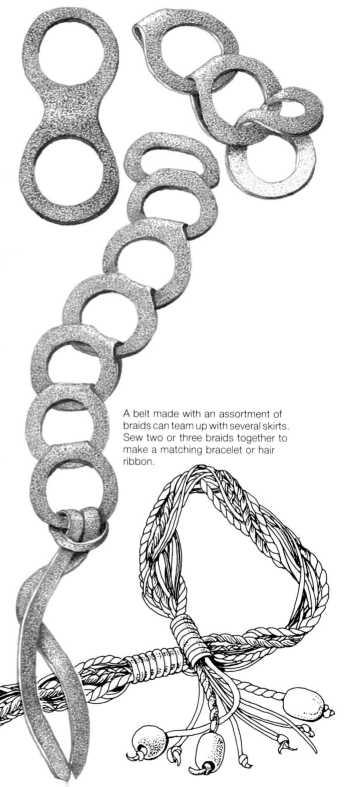

Before you start to cut out your links, make a paper template so that all the links are the same shape and size.

A belt made with an assortment of braids can team up with several skirts. Sew two or three braids together to make a matching bracelet or hair ribbon.

Make your own chess set

Pawn

Castle

Knight

Bishop

Queen

King

All chess sets must have 16 pawns, four castles, four knights, four bishops, two queens and two kings. Traditionally, half of these are painted white with the other half black or red to form two opposing sides.

Chess is a fascinating game and it's even more fun when played with pieces you have made yourself. The aim of the game is to capture as many of your opponent's pieces as possible so that ultimately you force the king into a tight spot from where he can't move without being captured. We haven't the space here to give all the rules of the game, but your local library will doubtless have a book on chess for beginners.

The most obvious material to use for your own set is self-hardening clay. You can base your design on the traditional sets, as illustrated at the top of the page, or you can look elsewhere for inspiration. There is a very famous set that was found on the Scottish Isle of Lewis and many replica sets have been produced. This was carved out of walrus ivory into simple solid shapes with the detail cut into it. So, self-hardening clay is a good medium to use as it, too, is hard-wearing but

Three pieces from the famous Isle of Lewis chess set. Made by the Vikings, this set is about 900 years old.

All chess boards are made up of 64 alternate black and white squares.

A simple wooden chess set. Illustrations can be cut from magazines or based on simple, stylized designs like the Egyptian one illustrated here.

soft enough to enable you to work on it once it has hardened. You can copy the Viking designs on the Isle of Lewis set or you can make up your own that will be totally unique.

Keep the larger pieces looking as different as possible or playing the game might prove difficult if there is any likelihood of confusing the pieces. You can choose any theme for your set as long as there are six easily distinguishable elements.

You could base your set simply on the "headgear" of the traditional set so the king would be a large crown, the queen would be a smaller crown, the bishop would be a mitre, the knight would be a medieval helmet with the vizor down, the castle would be the battlements of a castle keep and the pawns could be represented by simple medieval helmets.

Another possibility is to collect toy medieval figures, some on horseback and some on foot, decide which figures are to represent which pieces, glue them on to small wooden bases, then paint one set gold and the other silver.

Sets made out of small, flat pieces of wood are also hard-wearing and easy to play with. If wood is not readily available, sturdy cardboard could be used instead. Cut the wood into six different sizes so that the pawns are the shortest and the kings are the tallest. Choose a theme – we have illustrated an

Egyptian one here – and draw your pieces onto paper which can then be cut out and stuck onto the wood and laminated with clear sticky-backed film. Now glue your pieces to a wooden base or embed them in square pieces of self-hardening clay and leave to dry.

You can also make sets from papier mâché stuck onto a wire frame. Secure the wire frame to a small block of wood first so that the pieces are quite firm when you are playing with them. Cover the wire with several layers of papier mâché for a really strong figure.

Two contrasting chess pieces. The dumpy one below is made from self-hardening clay, while the more elegant figure is papier mâché on a wire frame.

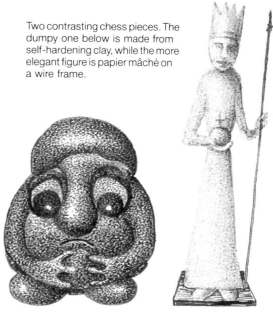

Cake creations

You can base your "cake creation" on any recipe as long as the cake is firm when you cut it. Some recipes result in a crumbly texture and these are best avoided. The "One-egg Cake" is a very quick and easy one to make and can be cooked in round or square pans or even in shallow swiss roll trays.

One-egg cake

2oz (50g) margarine	¼ tspoon salt
8oz (200g) sugar	2½ tspoons baking powder
1 egg	¼ pint (150 ml) milk
8oz (200g) flour	1 tspoon vanilla essence

Cream margarine and sugar together until light and fluffy. Add the egg and beat well. Sift the dry ingredients and add small amounts alternately with the milk. Pour into two shallow 9-inch pans. Bake in a moderate, pre-heated oven (180°C/350°F/Gas no. 4) for 25 minutes. When they are cooked, turn out onto cooling racks.

If you haven't time to make a cake, buy a plain sponge cake and use that instead.

Filling the cake

When the cake is completely cold, cut it in half and fill with one of the following:
1. Jam – apricot is particularly good.
2. Jam and cream, if it is to be eaten the same day.
3. Butter cream: cream together 2oz (50g) softened butter or soft margarine with 4oz (100g) sifted icing (confectioner's) sugar. Add 1 tablespoon of milk or a few drops of coffee, peppermint or almond essence. Alternatively, add a tablespoon of fruit juice instead of the milk.
4. Melted cooking chocolate: melt the chocolate as directed on the packet, then beat in 2oz (50g) butter or margarine.

Sandwich the two halves together. Make up the icing (confectioner's) sugar with a little warm water as directed on the packet. Pour the frosting onto the cake, smooth over and decorate.

CAKES IN ALL SHAPES AND SIZES

Clock Cake

Make up some white or yellow frosting and pour this all over the cake. Pipe on red figures, blue hands and brown minutes.

Hot Air Balloon

Use pale frosting for the background and decorate in any way you like, either with red, blue or green bands of frosting or use sugar

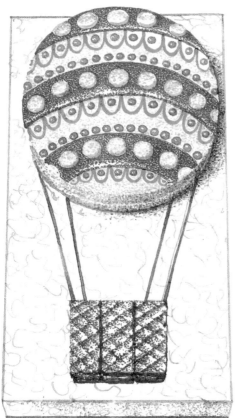

flowers and silver balls. Make the basket with wafers and dry spaghetti or liquorice laces for the connecting ropes.

Mother's Day Cake
Split and fill with jam and cream. Then turn your cake into a bright spring bonnet by first covering with pink or yellow frosting. Sit the cake on a large paper doily or several overlapping smaller ones so that they cover the edge of the plate and form the brim of the hat. Wind some matching ribbon around the side and cover the top with sugar flowers.

Race Track
Cover the cake with green frosting. Leave it to dry thoroughly. Then, using white frosting, pipe a winding circuit over the top of the cake. Finish off by putting small, plastic racing cars on the track.

Summertime Party Cake
Cut the cake into two or three layers. Fill each layer with thick cream and fresh strawberries, cut into slices. Decorate the top with more cream and strawberries, placed in a circular pattern. Simple, but delicious.

Square Cakes
These can easily be cut up and turned into something else or they can be decorated just as they are. A sport fanatic might like a football pitch, a tennis court or a golf course. An avid gardener might enthuse over a well-planned garden cake and a transport enthusiast would appreciate a car or a train.

Car Cake
Cut a square cake in half, then slice a small portion off one half. Put the shorter length on top of the other, cover with frosting and decorate. You could use pieces of chocolate for the windows and radiator grille and chocolate-chip cookies for the wheels.

Father's Day Cake
Cover the cake in blue or green frosting and place little edible silver balls in regular diagonal lines across the top and down the sides to give the effect of wrapping paper. Then pipe some "string" around the cake in red frosting to make it look like an attractive parcel. Finish off with a hand-written card, stuck into the middle of the cake saying, "To Dad, with love".

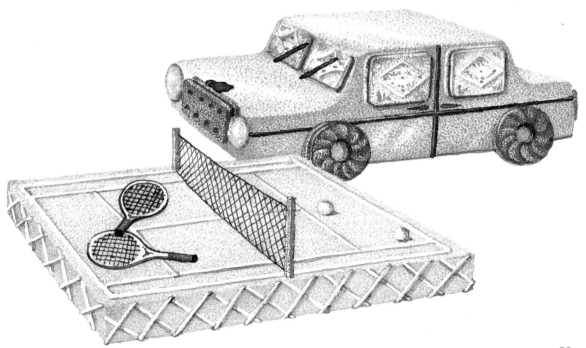

Pebbles and eggs

Pebbles and eggs are easy to paint and are fun to have around. Painted pebbles can be used as paperweights or simply as ornaments and they make cheap, attractive presents.

Ninety per cent of the effort involved in making a good decorated pebble needs to be put into thinking of an original subject and then planning the design.

PAINTED PEBBLES

A well-painted pebble on a stark white background looks very striking and "buyable". If you are making any for sale, remember to display them well, because it is a very important point in persuading people to buy them.

Acrylic paints are ideal, but you can use poster paints with a top coat of varnish.

What to paint

Furry curled-up animals lend themselves very well to this form of decorative art. You may need to look through several books on all sorts of subjects, before hitting on something that you really want to paint. For example, you could browse through books on natural history, pets and wild animals for natural forms, then books on fabric design, geology, gems and precious stones for abstract designs.

Plan the design on paper first; it's easier than trying to correct a mistake on the actual pebble.

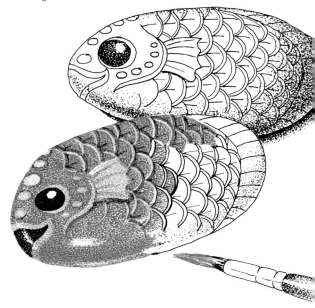

Your pebbles must be smooth and flat so collect some the next time you're on a pebbly beach. The shape of the pebble will occasionally suggest a design to you.

You need not restrict yourself to pebbles, though. Glass bottles and jars, painted with patterns or motifs, can be transformed into vases and containers.

DECORATED EGGS

You do need a certain lightness of touch when painting eggs. Free range eggs tend to have harder shells than most battery-produced ones so it's worth trying to get some of those.

Blown eggs keep longer than cooked eggs which do "go off" after a while. To prepare the egg, make a small hole with a darning needle at either end of the shell. You can make the holes larger with a skewer or clean knitting needle. Then, with a bowl underneath to catch the contents of the egg, blow down one end. You can always scramble the egg after or use it in an omelette. But don't make cakes with it as no one else will want to share them after you've blown all over the egg!

Rinse out the shell with warm water and leave to dry. If you want to close the holes up, lightly smear over some wall filler. You can decorate with paint or felt-tipped pen, but unless you are using acrylic paints you will need to apply a final coat of varnish which will not only give it a nice glossy finish, but will also strengthen it. The decorating will have to be done in two halves to allow the paint to dry. It's a good idea to hold the egg with a tissue to prevent the surface from becoming greasy or smudges occurring.

If you cook the egg first, allow it to cool before drawing the design on with felt-tipped pens. A dish of decorated eggs, cooked to accompany a salad, would look very attractive on the table at Easter.

Cold pre-cooked eggs, decorated with felt-tipped pens, make an eye-catching display at Easter. You can make very bold designs as intricate or as simple as you like. Even the youngest member of the family can help.

Competitive eggs

The next time your school holds a fête or fund-raising event, why not suggest that your class organizes a decorated egg competition? Ask all competitors to submit a decorated egg in an egg-cup, like the one illustrated above. This means they have to decorate only half an egg and the egg-cup itself can be used as part of the overall design.

Charge a small entry fee per egg and have two categories: the most decorative egg and the funniest.

Buy suitably eggs-citing prizes for the winners!

Badges

Badges can protest or support, be funny or decorative, but they always prove to be a talking point.

The materials you will need are some thin cardboard, a pair of scissors, paints or felt-tip pens, clear laminate, safety pins, sticky tape or sticky pads.

You can wear your badge unlaminated, but a covering of this sticky-backed clear film will protect it and give it a longer life.

Draw a circle on some thin cardboard using either a pair of compasses or an upturned wine glass. Now you have the size and shape of your badge, draw in the design you want. Use either one copied from a magazine or book or perhaps a slogan in support of something. Now decorate it, using paint or felt-tip pens, and cut it out.

Cut a circle from the laminate, 1in (2.5cm) wider in diameter than your original circle. Peel off the backing and place your badge, face down, in the middle of the circle of laminate. Now cut out notches all round the edge of this circle, as shown in the diagram on the left below. When all the notches are cut, bend the laminate over onto the back of the badge and press down. If you have any sticky pads you can use one of these on the back of the badge, otherwise fasten a safety pin there with some strong sticky tape.

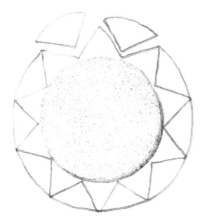

Make sure the badge is placed centrally on the piece of laminate. Cut notches out carefully.

Fold laminate over onto the back of the badge and attach a safety pin or a sticky pad.

Completed "plate of beans" badge.

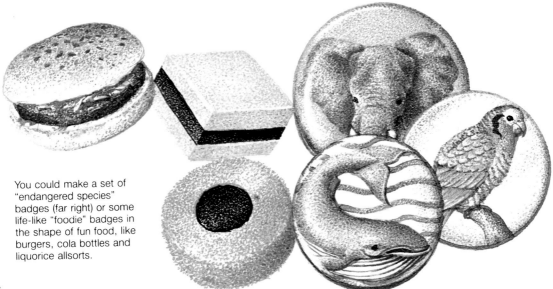

You could make a set of "endangered species" badges (far right) or some life-like "foodie" badges in the shape of fun food, like burgers, cola bottles and liquorice allsorts.

CLAY BADGES

You can also make badges out of self-hardening clay as it is very light and easy to wear, when dry.

Roll out a small piece of the clay, ⅛in (3mm) thick, and cut out the shape you want with a craft knife. You can build up detail on the surface of the badge once you have the outline cut out. The edges will soon begin to harden so you will have to work fairly quickly. Detail can also be added by using anything with a sharp point; a toothpick is ideal, but a nail file or even a small screwdriver would also work.

When the top looks dry, turn the badge over carefully so that the underside can dry out also. When you are certain that your badge is completely dry, paint on the details and features using an acrylic paint.

You can use sticky pads or a safety pin as before or you can embed the safety pin into the clay. If you wish to do this it must be done early on in the badge-making process. When you have cut out the shape then press the safety pin gently into the clay and smooth a little more clay over the top to make the pin really secure. Make sure it is the back of the pin that you have pushed into the clay or it won't open! Adding much detail to the front of the badge now has to be done with care.

Once the clay has hardened it is still possible to engrave extra detail into it with the point of a craft knife, and rough edges can be smoothed down with fine glasspaper.

Why not have a nice big spider climbing up your shirt, or make a really cuddly one out of fur-fabric?

When making the spider below, push some pieces of wire into the soft clay to give some nice spindly legs.

Pop-star badges are fun and you can change the picture as your taste changes!

57

Paper flowers

What better way of brightening up a dark corner of a room than by making a gorgeous overflowing vase of paper flowers? They are quick and easy to make and need just a few materials.

Gather together some bright crêpe or tissue paper, florists' wire, glue and scissors. You can invent your own petal shapes but there are a few basic designs that you can use to start with. When you've got the general idea you can then create exotic and unusual flowers of your own.

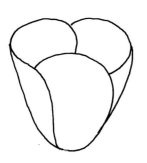  

1. Fold up the first shape quite tightly and glue the petals together so that they overlap.

2. Push some wire through the middle and turn the end over so that it will not pull back through

3. Continue to add petals onto the wire securing each one to the one before with a dab of glue at the base of the petal.

PEONIES

One of the easiest to begin with is the peony. Cut out ten or more three-petal shapes and then follow the step-by-step diagrams above.

Method

Bind thin strips of green crêpe paper around the wire to make it firmer and give it a more natural appearance. Now cut out two leaf shapes like the ones illustrated on the left and bind these to the stem with more paper-covered wire. These look super grouped together in a shallow bowl, particularly if you use different shades of pink, lilac and mauve or vibrant oranges, reds and yellows.

DAISIES

If your vase is going to stand against a wall then make a bunch of daisies. These can be made flat so that the detail is on one side only.

Method

Lightly draw a circle on some stiff tinted paper. Then pencil in the shape of the petals and cut around the edge. You now have the outer flower shape. Make a smaller shape to sit on top of it. Then make a shiny middle for your flower. Stitch a button to the three layers to secure them and prevent the paper from tearing. Attach a very thin dowel rod to the back of the flower with adhesive tape and bind it with green paper.

MAKING BUNCHES

Make several of these in different shades and use dowel rods of varying lengths so that you create a pleasing arrangement. If you think more "greenery" is needed, cut some long green leaf shapes and attach dowel rods to the backs of the leaves.

OTHER METHODS

Different shapes can be achieved by using individual petals cut in a variety of ways: heart shapes, pointed petals, rounded petals and even straight ones. Make each petal sufficiently long so that all the ends can be glued into each other, one at a time.

Or you could cut the petals from one long strip of crêpe paper. Fold it concertina-wise. Cut out a petal shape through all the layers, taking care not to snip right through the bottom edge. Unfold it, roll up loosely, tie the base with thread and fold back the petals. Wind the florists' wire around the base of the flower to make the stem.

Petals made in concertina strips.

Planting a tree

Most gardens, yards, patios or balconies, however small, are big enough to have at least one tree. Of course, the larger the space available, the bigger the tree you can have, but there are several dwarf varieties of trees, including fruit trees, that would grow well in a container on a patio or balcony.

If you have a very large area available and are very patient then you could try cultivating one of the broadleaved trees that grow to a great height like an oak or chestnut. It's best to start these off indoors by planting the acorn or chestnut in some moist peat in a good-sized pot. Place the pot in a dark, warm place until a green shoot appears, then put it on a sunny windowledge and keep well watered. When it is about 12-18in (30-45cm) high you can carefully transplant it out of doors. Do not plant it near the house, dividing wall or any other building because as it grows the roots will damage the foundations.

For most people a small to medium-sized tree is more suitable.

Choosing the tree

Do you want a tree that will give you a beautiful mass of blossom in the spring? If so,

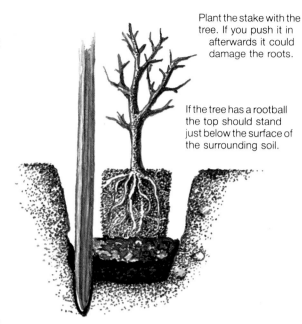

Plant the stake with the tree. If you push it in afterwards it could damage the roots.

If the tree has a rootball the top should stand just below the surface of the surrounding soil.

choose a lilac, flowering cherry or a fruit tree. Or do you want to see a display of brilliant tints later in the year? Then choose a Japanese maple or sumac tree. If you want to provide the birds with a plentiful supply of berries then an elder tree, mountain ash or cotoneaster would be the answer.

Position

All the trees mentioned here like a fairly sunny position, protected from cold winds. Most will do well in partial shade, but if you want masses of blossom or fruit then the sunnier the better.

Soil

When you buy your tree ask the dealer which soil the tree likes best. All of the trees on these two pages will grow happily in any reasonably fertile, well-drained soil.

Planting

Once you have bought your tree and chosen the position, you can prepare your tree for planting. If the tree has a rootball, with earth surrounding the root, water this well and leave to stand while you dig out the hole. If the roots are exposed, soak them in a bucket of water for approximately one hour.

Water the roots well before you plant the tree; this will give it a good start, particularly in dry weather.

Dig the hole about 18in (45cm) deep, depending on the size of the tree and its roots, and make the diameter twice as wide as the root spread or rootball. When the hole is large enough, loosen the earth inside to allow the roots to grow more easily, then spread some well-rotted garden compost or manure into the bottom of the hole. Carefully place the tree in the hole and, holding it upright, put the topsoil back in, smoothing it out well between the roots as you do so. If necessary, support the tree by tying it to a stake. When all the earth is back, firm it down gently with your foot. Then water well. If the soil is poor you can give your tree a liquid feed a month after planting and then once a month thereafter. Always keep the area surrounding trees free of weeds.

Containers

Japanese maple, strawberry tree, sumac, holly, cotoneaster, apple, plum and cherry are among the many trees that can be grown in containers. Make sure your container is large enough to allow for root growth, pack it well with soil and feed fortnightly. Water the pot at least once a day and twice during very hot weather. Trickle the water in slowly all around the edge of the pot and continue watering until it begins to flow from the base.

Continue to check all your trees regularly so that they are kept free of pests, are well-watered and the area surrounding them is kept weed-free.

If your tree gets "top heavy", it will become unstable, particularly in strong winds, so keep it well pruned.

A large tree needs lots of space, so choose your spot carefully!